Gratitude

This book belongs to

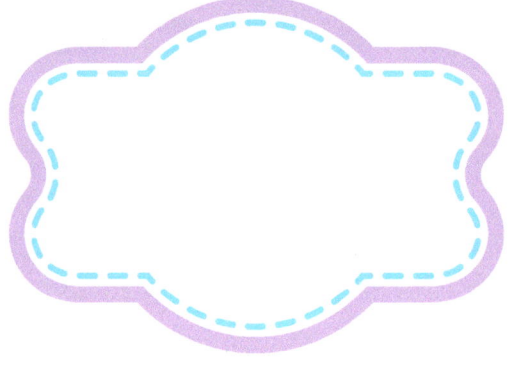

Gratitude

An Early Start to Learning the Positive Emotion of Gratitude

Sarah Hanley

© 2023 Sarah Hanley

All rights reserved. No part of this publication may be reproduced, distributed, or transmitted in any form or by any means, including photocopying, recording, or other electronic or mechanical methods, without the prior written permission of the publisher, except in the case of brief quotations embodies in critical reviews.

Book formatting by Gareth Southwell
art.garethsouthwell.com

Published by Spiritual Flow Publishing

ISBN (hardback): 978-1-7750273-3-1
ISBN (paperback): 978-1-7750273-2-4
ISBN (ebook): 978-1-7750273-4-8

This book is dedicated to each and everyone of you who have decided to explore this book and start your journey of discovering gratitude.

As you turn these pages, I hope that your heart embraces the magic of gratitude, bringing a smile to your face and allowing it to lead you on the path of happiness and creating the life you deserve.

Keep persevering!

Sarah

Gratitude.

You might have heard this word before, but let's explore what it truly means.

Gratitude is simply a fancy way of saying that you feel thankful or grateful for something.

It's a special feeling that fills your heart when someone does something nice for you or when you appreciate something they've done.

Gratitude is all about showing how much you appreciate the good things in your life, no matter how big or small they may be.

So, the next time you're enjoying your favorite snack, or enjoying a walk with your family, or even when a friend says something nice to you, take a moment to say "thank you" and feel the joy of gratitude!

Let's begin by creating a list of things you have to be grateful for in your life.

It might feel challenging at first, but the more you practice gratitude, the more things you will discover to be grateful for.

Gratitude not only makes you feel good, but there's actually a scientific reason behind it.

When you express gratitude, it activates the release of feel-good chemicals in your brain, such as dopamine and serotonin.

These chemicals work together to boost your mood and contribute to a greater sense of happiness.

It's like receiving a free dose of happiness every time you say "thank you"!

Gratitude can also help you sleep better.

When you take time to appreciate the good things in your life before bed, it can help calm your mind and reduce stress, leading to a more restful sleep.

So, say "thank you" before you tuck yourself in at night!

thank ♡ you

When you express gratitude, it can make your relationships better.

Showing appreciation for the people in your life helps you become closer to them and makes them feel extra special.

DREAM BIG

One of the best things about gratitude is that it can help you achieve your goals.

By appreciating the positive things in your life, it makes you feel excited and ready to go after your dreams.

Gratitude can be like a helpful push that supports you along the way.

You can do a few things to have more gratitude in your life.

Every day you should set aside a few minutes to think about things you are grateful for.

You can write them down in a journal or you can say them in your mind.

When you think about what you're grateful for, try to appreciate what you have right now.

It's easy to think about things from the past or what you want in the future, but being in the moment and paying attention to the good things happening around you will create space for more things to be grateful for.

Be specific when expressing gratitude.

Instead of just saying you're grateful for your family, think about a special moment or something kind they did that made you feel grateful.

When you are specific it makes it more meaningful and special!

Let's take three things you are grateful for and be specific!

For example, you can be grateful for the time your brother helped you clean your room or when your mom made your favorite meal.

1. _____

2. _____

3. _____

Even when things are hard, it's important to practice gratitude.

Always try to find something positive to be grateful for.

It can change how you see the situation and make you feel better.

An example of a situation where you can chose gratitude over negative thoughts would be if your parent or guardian cleaned your room, but you're upset because they touched your things.

Instead of getting mad, why not be grateful for having a clean room? It feels great to be in a clean space where everything is organized!

Appreciate how nice it was of your parent to do that for you. Let's focus on the positive and be thankful for their help!

Remember, it's important to share your gratitude with others!

You can write a thank-you note, tell someone in person how much you appreciate them, or even give them a small gift.

You can also show gratitude by cooking a meal for someone or planning an outdoor activity together.

Another fun idea is to create a gratitude jar. All you need is a jar and some small pieces of paper.

Whenever you feel grateful, write it down on a piece of paper and put it in the jar.

At the end of the month or year, you can read through all the notes and think about all the good things in your life.

It's a great way to reflect on your gratitude!

Gratitude is like a universal language that everyone can understand, no matter where they come from or what they believe in.

Gratitude helps you connect with others and brings everyone closer together.

When you start noticing and appreciating all the wonderful things around you, you become a master of gratitude!

Let's embrace the magic of gratitude and spread happiness wherever you go!

About the Author

Over the last year, Sarah embarked on a transformative journey of self-love, which lead to a desire to share the valuable lessons she was learning with her children. With her books, her ultimate goal is to provide children with the necessary tools and inspiration to become the best versions of themselves. Through her writing, Sarah aspires to guide young readers towards embracing their unique qualities, fostering self-love, and empowering them with the confidence to navigate life's challenges.

Books

 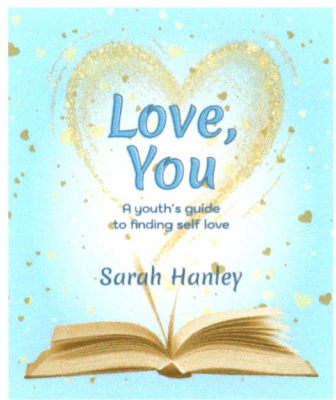 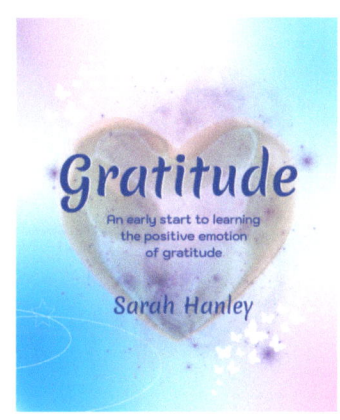

Journals

 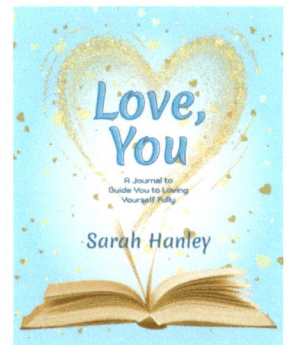 

www.ingramcontent.com/pod-product-compliance
Lightning Source LLC
Chambersburg PA
CBHW042251100526
44587CB00002B/101